Sleep is a great healer. It regenerates your body, clears emotional conflicts, and helps you think and work at peak efficiency. That is, as long as you get enough of it. A lot of people don't. So how much sleep is enough? Some people get by quite well on five or six hours per night, while others require a full eight hours. The amount of sleep you need is an individual matter, so it is impossible to make hard and fast rules about it. The better your diet—the higher it is in fresh fruits and vegetables and natural, unprocessed foods—and the more exercise you get daily, the less time you are likely to need to sleep.

By Leslie Kenton
Published by Ivy Books:

BEAT STRESS
BOOST ENERGY
GET FIT
LOOK GREAT
LOSE FAT
SLEEP DEEP

SLEEP DEEP

Leslie Kenton

IVY BOOKS · NEW YORK

Ivy Books
Published by Ballantine Books
Copyright © 1996 by Leslie Kenton

http://www.randomhouse.com

Library of Congress Catalog Card Number: 96-94974

ISBN 0-8041-1627-X

Manufactured in the United States of America

First American Edition: March 1997

10 9 8 7 6 5 4 3 2 1

Contents

Author's Note

The material in this book is intended for information purposes only. None of the suggestions or information is meant to be prescriptive. Any attempt to treat a medical condition should always come under the directions of a competent physician. Readers should always consult with a health care professional before starting a new diet or exercise program. Neither the publisher nor I can accept responsibility for injuries or illness arising out of a failure by a reader to take medical advice. I am only a reporter. I also have a profound interest in helping myself and others maximize our potential for positive health.

SLEEP

DEEP

Introduction

Sleep is a great healer. It regenerates your body, clears emotional conflicts, and helps you think and work at peak efficiency. That is, as long as you get enough of it. A lot of people don't. In Britain alone 50 million sleeping pills are swallowed each year, which means that for every person addicted to narcotics there are twelve hooked on barbiturates.

So how much sleep is enough? Some people get by quite well on five or six hours per night, while others require a full eight hours. The amount of sleep you need is an individual matter, so it is impossible to make hard and fast rules about it. The better your diet—the higher it is in fresh fruits and vegetables and natural, unprocessed foods—and the more exercise you get daily, the less time you are likely to need to sleep.

What matters most is not the duration of your night's sleep, but rather its quality. High-quality sleep does not mean drugging yourself into oblivion. For overnight re-energizing, you must let go completely and surrender yourself to the wonderfully enriching experience of blissful sleep.

CHAPTER 1

What Is Sleep?

Much about sleep remains a mystery in spite of all the elaborate research that has been done into how and why we sleep and dream. And most of the common notions about sleep are untrue. For instance, sleep is not some kind of "little death" from which you are rescued every morning. Nor do you go to bed to fall deeper and deeper into sleep until you reach bottom somewhere after midnight, after which you come closer and closer to consciousness until you finally awaken. Also, deep sleep is not any more beneficial than light sleep. And we do not necessarily need the obligatory eight hours a night to remain stress-wise and well.

Two Faces of Sleep

There are two kinds of sleep: *orthodox* sleep, which is dreamless—sometimes called synchronized slow-wave sleep because of the brain wave patterns that accompany it—and *paradoxical* sleep, during which dreaming occurs along with rapid eye movement (REM)—sometimes called desynchronized sleep. Orthodox sleep is vital for physical restoration of the body while paradoxical sleep is essential to your mental and emotional stability. Research into sleep measured by electroencephalograms has shown that all of us spend our sleep time moving in and out of these two types of sleep in predictable rhythmic patterns. If for any reason these patterns are repeatedly disturbed, we suffer.

There are four levels or depths to orthodox sleep. When you fall asleep you move into the first level, characterized by low-amplitude fast-frequency brain wave patterns. Sometimes sleep starts with a sudden twitching movement called a myoclonic jerk. This is the result of a sudden flare-up of electrical activity in the brain, as in a minor epileptic seizure. Then, as you move to level two and even deeper into levels three and four, there is a general slowing of the frequency and an increase in the amplitude of your brain waves.

Normally you fall asleep and remain for a short time at levels one and two and then plunge into levels three and four to stay there for seventy to one hundred minutes. At that point comes your first period of REM, or paradoxical, sleep when dreams begin. This dream period of REM lasts only ten to twenty minutes. It is repeated again at about ninety-minute intervals throughout the night with orthodox, undreaming, sleep in between, culminating in the longest period of REM—usually about half an hour—just before you wake up.

During orthodox sleep your body is quiet, heartbeat slows, blood pressure falls slightly, and your breathing gets slower and more regular. Even your digestive system winds down. In the deeper levels of orthodox sleep, brain waves gradually become more synchronized, as if everything is at peace. At such times your body's restorative processes come into their own, rapidly repairing damaged tissues and cells, producing antibodies to fight infection, and carrying out a myriad of other duties necessary to keep you healthy. Without orthodox sleep in all its different stages, this important vegetative restoration does not take place properly and you become more prone to stress-damage, illness, early aging, fatigue, and muddled thinking. Orthodox sleep is the master restorer.

Pure Contradiction

REM sleep, which is diametrically opposite to orthodox sleep in many ways, is just as vital. It more than earns the name "paradoxical" by being a mass of contradictions: although the body is virtually paralyzed during the REM state, the fingers and face often twitch and in men the penis may become erect. Breathing speeds up to the level of your normal waking state. Heartbeat rate, blood pressure, and temperature rise, and adrenaline shoots through the system. Beneath the lids your eyes move rapidly from side to side as though you were looking at a film or tennis match. And this is exactly what is happening—you are viewing images that come rapidly in succession. Your brain waves in the REM state show a marked similarity to the rapid, irregular patterns of being awake.

Although the exact purpose of REM sleep remains a mystery, researchers know that it is essential for maintaining one's mental and emotional equilibrium. The need for paradoxical sleep also varies from one person to another. How much you will need is related to both your personality and your general psychological state. Longer periods of REM sleep and more of them throughout the night take place in times of psychic pain, or when your defense patterns are being challenged by new demands. Women tend to have increased REM sleep during the three or four days before the beginning of a period. For most women this is a time of increased anxiety, irritability, mood changes, and unstable defense patterns. But there is a lot that is not known about the function of paradoxical sleep. Well-known French researcher Michel Jouvet, who has done extensive studies of the REM state in animals and their unborn young—in which it occurs as well—believes it is a kind of practice of the genetic code in which lower animals run through their instinctive behavior patterns. In mammals and man, he thinks, it is a time when we are probably practicing our learned behavior as each night we go through the process of integrating new information with the knowledge we already have.

Psychic Necessity

When animals are deprived of REM sleep they become increasingly excitable, their appetite soars, a disturbed sexuality appears, and eventually they suffer a nervous breakdown. Studies also show that even too little REM makes them more and more restless and anxious. Their short-term memory starts to fail and they suffer from poor concentration and other unpleasant symptoms. Sleep researchers have discovered this by watching carefully and waking up their subjects each time they enter the paradoxical stage of sleep—indicated by rapid eye movements clearly visible beneath closed eyelids.

This aspect of REM sleep is particularly interesting, for when scientists disturb sleepers in the orthodox state, they find that deprivation of orthodox sleep doesn't lead to any psychological disturbances. But after being deprived of REM sleep for several days, however, sleepers become desperate for it. Their normal sleep patterns alter so that they slip into REM immediately on falling asleep and then experience twenty to thirty periods of it each night instead of the usual three. Psychologists refer to this phenomenon as "REM rebound." It is often accompanied by fierce nightmares as psychic imagery, too long repressed, seeks strongly to reassert itself.

Sleeping pills repress this REM phase, and repression can result in lasting psychological damage to the pill popper. After taking sleep-inducing drugs regularly, when you come off them you may fear you are going crazy as you start to experience the REM rebound. Vivid and frightening hypnagogic images and nightmares appear as the body hungrily tries to make up for what it has been denied. There are other reasons to steer clear of sleep-inducing drugs too. Both barbiturates and nonbarbiturates prescribed for sleep are physically and psychologically addictive—barbiturates to an even greater degree than heroin. They can be fatal, even at low dosage, when mixed with alcohol in the bloodstream. Finally— something that few people realize—they are also not very effective over the long term.

Sleeping pills can be successfully used to bring on sleep only for the first week or two. After that, dangerously increased doses are needed to work. For many people who rely on sleeping pills, the power of suggestion brought about by putting one in the mouth and swallowing it is far more useful than the drug in introducing sleep. The drug itself can only do harm in the long run; sleeping pills themselves put your body under continual stress. There are safer and more effective ways of getting to sleep.

How Much Sleep?

The amount of sleep you need varies tremendously from one person to another. It also varies from one day to the next. There is no truth in the idea that you need eight hours of sleep to stay well and feel energetic. You might need ten hours, while another person gets on very well with four and a half. One study showed that short sleepers tend to be active, outgoing people who are sociable, flexible in their personalities, and more conformist socially. Those wanting longer periods of sleep are more introverted and creative and are particularly good at sustained work. Often the more stress-filled your day, the more sleep you will need to balance it.

As we get older we tend to sleep less. Many sixty- and seventy-year-olds get by on a mere three or four hours a day. Occasionally you meet someone who sleeps as little as half an hour to an hour each night, yet appears to be perfectly normal. The amount of sleep you need depends so much on your biological and psychological individuality that you can't make hard and fast rules about it. Many high achievers and great minds throughout history—Napoleon, Freud, and Thomas Edison, for instance—have been poor sleepers, while others, such as Einstein, could sleep the day away. But the idea that you need a certain amount of sleep each night to stay well is a powerful one. For many people it is so embedded in their unconscious that if they get only seven hours one night instead of eight, they are convinced they will be tired the next day and soon develop all the signs of it. If you are one of these people, try re-examining your premises, and experiment—sleep less and see what happens. You may find that how you feel after a certain amount of sleep depends more on your own choice than on the time spent in bed. Try sleeping less for a few days. Many people find when they do, they actually have *more* energy.

CHAPTER 2

Forget Insomnia

A lot of so-called insomnia is nothing more than the result of worrying about getting to sleep. Many people who consider themselves insomniacs are really victims of general propaganda about sleep rather than true non-sleepers. And many people seek treatment because they can sleep only four or five hours a night, although that may be all they need. There is nothing more apt to cause sleeplessness than the worry that you won't be able to drop off. Sometimes sleeplessness can be normal. After all, we all experience a sleepless night now and then, particularly if we are overtired, worried, or excited about some coming event.

Real, chronic insomnia is less frequent. A

major research project into long-term insomnia turned up some interesting facts about sufferers. Over 85 percent of the 300 insomniacs studied had one or more major pathological personality indications, such as depression, obsessive compulsive tendencies, schizophrenic characteristics, or sociopathy. For them, their insomnia was a secondary symptom of a more basic conflict. Insomnia was a socially acceptable problem they could talk about without fear of being judged harshly. Insomnia is little more than a mask for whatever is really bothering the nonsleeper. Occasionally the inability to sleep can be a manifestation of a nutritional problem—often a deficiency in zinc coupled with an excess of copper, which produces a mind that is intellectually overactive and won't wind down—or a deficiency of calcium, magnesium, or vitamin E, which can lead to tension and cramping in the muscles and a difficulty in letting go.

The more easygoing an attitude you have toward sleep, the less likely you are to have any problem with it. If you miss an hour or two, or if you are not sleepy, simply stay up, read a book, or finish some work. Believe it or not, one of the best times for coming up with creative ideas is in the middle of a sleepless night. It can be the perfect opportunity for turning stress into something creative. Chances are that you'll more than make up for it in the next couple of days—provided you don't get anxious about it.

Insomnia is one of women's greatest fears. Eight times more women report sleep difficulties to their doctors throughout their lives than do men. Apart from the motherhood-induced insomnia that comes from having to feed a baby, if ever you are going to have trouble sleeping it is most likely to be during the perimenopausal years just before your periods stop or much later on in your seventies and eighties. People sleep less as they get older for a number of reasons, not the least of which is a decrease in the production of a substance called melatonin, which regulates the body's circadian rhythms. How much sleep you need can change depending on your life circumstances, too. When you are pregnant, eat less wholesome foods, or are under stress or ill, you may need more sleep. You need more sleep when you gain weight, too. When losing weight, or during a detoxification regime, you will often sleep less.

The sleeplessness that occurs in women around the time of menopause and in the few

years just before is usually not a difficulty in
going to sleep but a tendency to awaken regularly at the same time each night (usually two
or three in the morning) and to lie in bed wide
awake. Because we are accustomed to sleeping
through the night, we assume that there must
be something wrong. Yet sleeplessness can
sometimes bring new insights, if you are ready
to receive them. Many artists, writers, and
composers will tell you that they receive inspi-
ration for new projects and discover ways of
overcoming creative challenges on awakening
in the night.

Common Treatment

Nevertheless, when sleeplessness becomes
chronic it can leave you feeling exhausted,
hopeless, and washed out, in which case something needs to be done about it. Sleeping pills
are not the answer. Their side effects include
digestive problems, poor concentration, disorders of the blood and respiration, high blood
pressure, liver and kidney troubles, problems
with vision, depression, dizziness, confusion,

and damage to the central nervous system. Using them can even lead to worse insomnia. There are better ways.

How—and How Not—to Get to Sleep

Next time you are troubled by sleeplessness take a look at nature's sleep aids.

• Begin each day with twenty minutes in the sun or in very bright light. Your circadian rhythms are linked to sunlight. The sun sets our natural clocks properly and acts as a natural energizer too.

• Get more exercise regularly during the day. This helps burn up stress-caused adrenaline buildup in the brain, which can result in that tense, nervous feeling that you are "up" and can't seem to get "down." Experiment with exercising at different times of the day to see which time works best for you in terms of relaxing you and making you ready for sleep at night. But don't do strenuous exercise before going to bed, as it can set the heart pounding and stimulate the whole body too much.

• Don't take on any new activities late in the day and don't take a nap in the evening or late afternoon.

• Don't eat dinner late in the evening—the earlier the better. Make it the smallest meal of the day and avoid snacks after dinner since they can interfere with sleep. Everybody sleeps better on an empty stomach, despite what the hot drink manufacturers would have you believe.

• Don't drink coffee, alcohol, or strong stimulants at dinner. This isn't just an old wives' tale. One researcher looking into the effects of caffeine on human beings recently showed that total sleep time is decreased by two hours and the mean total of intervening wakefulness more than doubles when patients are given three milligrams of caffeine, the equivalent of a couple of cups of coffee. Alcohol may put you to sleep but it tends not to keep you there, awakening you instead in the early hours of the morning.

- Drink milk. It is an old-fashioned remedy, maybe, but scientifically sound: drinking a glass of milk before bed helps you to sleep. Milk contains tryptophan, a precursor to one of the calming brain chemicals, called serotonin, which is important for relaxation and for inducing sleep. And it is high in calcium, which is often referred to as the slumber mineral because it induces muscle relaxation.

- Drink plenty of water during the day. Sleep is induced by the brain, and brain cells need adequate hydration both to stay awake during the daylight hours and to trigger the dreamy relaxation that brings on sleep. Hardly anyone drinks as much water as they profitably could. I regularly consume at least two quarts of mineral water a day in addition to whatever other drinks I may have.

- Don't go to bed when you are not sleepy. Instead, pursue some pleasant activity, preferably passive. Television is not the best choice, for some researchers believe the electromagnetic radiation TV sets emit may disturb your nervous system when you least need it.

· Get into a rut, going to bed as close as possible to the same time every night and developing a routine or simple ritual about it. When it comes to getting ready for sleep each night, the body loves routines; they foster relaxation and let the body know what to expect. Make bedtime and rising time as regular as possible and go through the same routine each evening of putting the cat out, opening the window, reading a book, etc.

· Soak in a lukewarm (not hot) bath for thirty minutes, adding hot water to maintain the temperature at just blood heat. (A hot bath before bed is a mistake. It is far too stimulating to the heart and gets your motor running.) Blot your skin dry without friction and go straight to bed, moving slowly. This can be a great thing to do in the middle of the night if you awaken too—use a candle instead of turning on the light and let yourself relax as you probably never can during the day when a telephone could ring or someone might demand something of you.

- Insist that you sleep in a room by yourself if you want to be alone. Nights, sometimes weeks, of sleeping alone can be enormously restful and fruitful.

- Use an ionizer, a little contraption you can keep beside your bed that sends negative ions into the air and is a godsend to anyone who has the kind of nervous system that tends to go "up" and doesn't want to come "down." Although not cheap, it is an excellent investment, for you can use it at a desk when you have a lot of work to do. Or, if you buy one of the portable varieties, you can also take it in the car on long trips to keep you from going to sleep (it magically works both ways) and on flights to minimize the effects of jet lag. Negative ions also stimulate the production of serotonin in the brain.

- Listen to mellow music. Music too can help alter consciousness and have you sinking blissfully into the depths of slumber. A

Walkman with a few tapes by the side of your bed is one of the most pleasant ways of all of putting a racing mind to rest and easing yourself into sleep.

• Some of the essential plant oils have a wonderful calming effect on the mind and body. You can take a warm bath with them or place a few drops on your pillow to inhale through the night. For the bath use four drops of lavender oil, two drops of chamomile, and two drops of neroli (orange blossom). Or try a drop or two of each on your pillow.

• Count your blessings. It's an old-fashioned idea but it is a true key to deep relaxation and blissful sleep. Each night as you turn out the light, think of six things during the day that you have to be thankful for, regardless of your physical or emotional state or how difficult your life may be at the time. This gradually turns the mind to dwell on pleasurable themes even when you are awake. It can even improve the quality of your dreams.

- Make use of the following relaxation techniques and helpers—you will find they enhance many other areas of your life too.

Stop worrying about getting to sleep. Just let it happen. If it doesn't tonight, so what? It will tomorrow night. Or the next. Lack of sleep is not going to kill you, but worrying about it long enough just might.

CHAPTER 3

Relax

A good night's sleep, as Shakespeare knew, can "knit up the ravell'd sleeve of care." The problem is that sleep is not something you can *try* to get. No amount of wishing and wanting can guarantee peaceful repose. Sleeping involves a mode that many people know little about—*allowing* rather than doing. The following are some helpful ways of learning to let go, to soften and allow, to help you to encourage the mode of sleep.

Release Stress

We live in a world of striving and goals, of planning and remembering—a world of never-ending sensory stimulation, ideas, and discoveries. Yet amid all this activity somewhere inside you is a center of stillness—a wordless, formless space—the home of your self or your soul. There seeds of creativity are sown that later become your ideas and your accomplishments. There in the silence and the darkness you can begin to listen to your own inner voice. You can come to know the difference between what you really want, feel, and think, and what has been programmed into you by habits, false notions, and other people's values. This space—your center—is also a place of safety and security. You can move out of it, as you choose, to meet the outside world, form friendships, love, and learn. Yet it is a permanent sanctuary to which you can always return when you feel overburdened, tired, confused, or in need of new vitality and direction. The key that opens this particular door for most of us is relaxation.

Passive Awareness

By relaxation I mean learning to move at will into a state of deep stillness in which your usual concerns, your habitual thoughts, and the never-ending activity of your daily life are replaced by alert—yet totally passive—awareness. Dipping into such a state even for a few minutes allows many of the physiological changes normally experienced during sleep to take place while your body and mind are revitalized. But it is different from sleep. For while your body is passive, your mind is highly alert.

For some people this state occurs spontaneously—often between sleep and wakefulness. It is during this time that their best ideas come and that they experience a sense of harmony both within themselves and in relation to the rest of the world. Most of us, however, have a fear of letting go, thinking that if we give up control of things we won't be able to think clearly and independently or work well, or that someone is likely to put something over on us. In fact, just the opposite is true. When you are able to enter a state of deep relaxation at will, this frees you from patterns of living

and thinking to which you tend to be a slave—
although usually an unconscious one. It enables
you to think more clearly and simply and to act
more directly when action is called for.

Another interesting benefit derived from the
daily practice of deep relaxation is a reduction
of negative habits such as drug taking—of
both prescription and mind-altering drugs—
alcohol consumption, and cigarette smoking.
Research carried out in the United States
involving 2,000 students between the ages of
nineteen and twenty-three who had practiced a
form of meditation for periods of a few months
to a couple of years showed that their depen-
dence on alcohol, drugs, and cigarettes dropped
sharply. The number of smokers was reduced
by half in the first six months of doing the
practice. By twenty-one months it was down to
one-third. And these changes were entirely
spontaneous—at no time was any suggestion
made that relaxation or meditation would
change any of these habits.

Harvard professor and expert in behavioral
medicine Herbert Benson, M.D., did the first
studies into the effects of transcendental meditation many years ago. He has since continued
to investigate this state of psychophysical
relaxation and has shown that each of us

has what he calls the "relaxation response"—a
natural ability to experience the relaxed state
with all its benefits. All we need to tap into it
is a method to turn it on. The possibilities
are many. They range from meditation, yoga,
breathing exercises, zazen, silent repetition
of a word, and autogenic training, to steady
aerobic exercise and biofeedback. Each can be
useful as a tool for silencing everyday thoughts
and for temporarily shutting off habitual ways
of seeing the world and doing things. Practice
one of these methods regularly and you build a
powerful and useful bridge between your inner
and outer world. All of them are different.
Some will work better for you or be more enjoy-
able than others. That is why it is worthwhile
to try a few different techniques until you discover which ones you prefer.

Discipline for Freedom

We live in an age when discipline is often
looked down upon as something that interferes
with spontaneity and freedom—something old-
fashioned and stifling to life. We tend to rebel

against it. But the kind of discipline needed for daily practice of meditation or deep relaxation tends—far from stifling one's ability to be involved in the spontaneous business of life— actually to free it. This is something you will have to find out for yourself. At first it may take a little effort to get up fifteen or twenty minutes earlier each morning to practice a technique and to take fifteen minutes out of your busy afternoon or early evening to practice again, but you will find it is well worth it. The most common excuse is that you don't have time. The reality of the situation is that practicing twice a day for fifteen or twenty minutes will *give* you time, not take it from you, for you will find that you do everything with greater efficiency and enjoyment, and that far less of your energy is wasted on fruitless activity. Studies show that every minute you spend in a deeply relaxed state yields a fourfold return in the energy you have in your outer life.

Progressive Relaxation

A technique based on the work of Edmund Jacobson, this is an excellent way to begin if you have never done any sort of relaxation or meditation technique before, because it gives most people some sense of what relaxation feels like even the first time you try it. As you repeat your technique (it is best done for fifteen minutes at least twice a day), you will find you enter a state of relaxation that is progressively deeper and deeper.

The first few times you try the technique, you may find you have trouble picturing all the images as they come or preventing your mind from wandering. It doesn't matter if you don't "see" anything—some people are more visual in their imagery and others more feeling; both work superbly well—just approach the exercise from your own point of view. When you find your mind wandering (this is a common occurrence because your concentration is not used to focusing so intensely, or because you are experiencing something new to you, which naturally enough causes a little anxiety) ask yourself, "Why is my mind wandering?" Pursue that thought for a couple of minutes, then go back to the exercise and continue to go through it as best you can. All difficulties will iron themselves out automatically after you have practiced the technique long enough—so persevere to overcome any initial difficulties.

- Find a quiet room, preferably one without too much light, and sit in a comfortable chair that supports your back. Place both feet flat on the floor and close your eyes.

- Become aware of your breathing and just let the air come in and out of your body without doing anything.

- Take a few deep breaths. Each time you breathe out, slowly repeat the word *relax* silently to yourself.

- Focus on your face and let yourself feel any tension in your face or eyes, your jaw or tongue. Make a mental picture of tension—you could picture a clenched fist, a knotted rope, or a hard ball of steel—then mentally picture the tension going and everything becoming relaxed, like a limp rubber band.

- Feel your face and your eyes, your jaw and your tongue becoming relaxed, and as they relax, experience a wave of relaxation spreading through your whole body. (Each step takes about ten seconds.)

- Tighten up all the muscles in your face and eyes, squeezing them as hard as you can. Then let go and feel the relaxation spread throughout your body again.

- Now apply the same instruction to other parts of your body, moving slowly downward from your head to your neck, shoulders, and upper back, arms, hands, chest, mid and lower back, abdomen, thighs, calves, ankles, feet, and toes, going through each area until every part of your body is relaxed. With each part, picture the tension in it mentally and then picture it going away; each time, tense the muscles in that area and then let them go and feel the relaxation spreading.

- When you've relaxed every part of your body, sit quietly in this comfortable state for up to five minutes.

- Now let the muscles in your eyelids become lighter; get ready to open your eyes and come back to an awareness of the room.

- Open your eyes. Now you are ready to do whatever you want to do.

Core–Connections

A daily meditation practice gives access to energy resources from deep within through the process of allowing. Regular meditation helps improve your concentration and focus so that you are able to pour all of yourself into whatever activity you undertake. Anyone who has erratic energy ups and downs and mood swings can benefit considerably from meditating for fifteen to thirty minutes a day.

The traditional way to meditate is sitting cross-legged on a cushion on the floor. (Raising your bottom a few inches off the ground helps align the spine and is more comfortable.) You may find it helpful to adopt the Buddhist practice of placing the back of the left hand in the palm of the right one, and it is often helpful to meditate in the same place each time.

Zazen

One of the simplest ways of meditating, this technique involves nothing more than just being aware of your breathing. But don't be deceived by its simplicity. It is a potent tool for stilling the mind and regenerating the body. And concentrating your awareness on the breath is not as easy as it sounds.

• Find yourself a quiet place where you will not be disturbed. You can sit cross-legged on the floor with a small cushion underneath you or you can sit in a chair if you prefer, but your back should be straight. (This straight-back position is a requirement for many meditation techniques, since it creates a physical equilibrium that makes calm mental focus possible.) Let your hands rest quietly in your lap.

- Close your eyes. Take several long, slow breaths, breathing from your abdomen so it swells out with each in-breath and sinks in again when you breathe out.

- Now rock your body from side to side and then around in large, gentle circles from your hips to the top of your head. Rock in increasingly smaller circles until you gradually come to rest in the center.

- Now breathe in and out through your nose quietly without doing anything to your breathing—that is, don't try to breathe deeper or slower or faster, just breathe normally. With each out-breath count silently to yourself. So it goes: in-breath, out-breath "one" . . . in-breath, out-breath "two" . . . and so on up to ten, counting only on the out-breath. When you get to ten go back and begin again at one. If you lose count halfway, it doesn't matter. Go back and start the count at one again. Counting isn't the point. It is a way of focusing your mind on your breath.

  If you are like most people, the first few times you do the exercise you will find you lose count often and are frequently distracted by thoughts or noises. It makes no difference.

It works just as well anyway. Each time some random thought distracts you, simply turn your mind gently back again to counting the breaths. Distractions don't change the effectiveness of the meditation.

- After fifteen minutes—sneak a look at your wristwatch if you must—stop. Sit still for a moment, then open your eyes and slowly begin your everyday activities again.

The exercise, like most techniques, is best done twice a day, morning and evening. A beginner will usually notice positive results by the end of a week but they become increasingly apparent the longer you go on doing it. Some Buddhist monks do this exercise for two or three years before beginning any other form of meditation.

Beyond Relaxation

Once you are familiar with the practice of deep relaxation or meditation and with all the benefits it can bring you, you might be interested to go on to investigate other, more complex forms of meditation. There are many, for meditation is not a word that is easy to define. It takes in such different practices. Some forms, such as zazen or vispassana (sometimes called insight meditation), demand complete immobility. You sit watching the rise and fall of your abdomen as you breathe, and whenever your mind wanders you gently turn it back to this observation. This simply concentrated attention, which can be likened to the "continuum of awareness" in Gestalt theory, is capable of bringing up many repressed feelings and thoughts that have been stifling your full expression and of liberating them. The Siddha Yoga of Muktananda and the chaotic meditation of Rajneesh in which the body is let go to move as it will are examples of this sort. They often involve spontaneous changes in muscle tension and relaxation and in breathing, and demand a surrender to the physical body for the release of mental, emotional, and bodily tensions. These kinds of meditation can be particularly good for someone with a tendency to be physically rigid.

A Breath of Medicine

When sleeplessness arises out of anxiety or
brings worries in its wake it can be useful to
shift the focus of your energy toward the
breath using one of the most simple yet powerful techniques I know from yogic breathing.
Practice it first when you are relaxed so you
know it well. You can then call on it not only
during sleepless nights to transform your anxious energy into calm but also at any time
during the day when you may feel worried or
feel a sense of panic coming on about anything.
Sitting straight in a chair or with your legs
crossed on a cushion on the floor—once you get
the hang of it you can do this exercise lying
down as well—place the tip of your tongue on
the ridge of your palate just behind your front
teeth. Keep it there during the whole of the
exercise. Breathe out completely through your
mouth, pursing your lips a bit if necessary and
letting the air move out around your tongue (it
makes a soft whooshing sound). Now you are
ready to begin:

- Close your mouth and silently inhale through the nose to a count of four.

- Hold your breath to a count of seven.

- Now exhale fully through your mouth, again making a *whoosh* sound as you do so, to a count of eight.

- Repeat the whole of the above four times.

The in-breath is taken silently through the nose with the mouth closed and the out-breath, which takes twice as long, is made through the slightly opened mouth. How much time you spend on each phase of the breath is up to you. In the beginning it is likely to be faster, and later on when you have used the exercise a lot it is likely to slow down a great deal. This really does not matter. What is important is that you maintain the same 4:7:8 ratio during the whole exercise and that your tongue remains on the ridge just behind your upper teeth. According to yogic theory, there are two kinds of energy in the human body—positive and negative nerve currents—one being solar and the other lunar. They begin and end at this spot behind the upper front teeth and at the tip of the tongue. By putting the two together you are completing a circuit that enables you to hold the power of breath energy, so restoring balance and serene well-being.

After you have learned this exercise and used it for a few weeks, you can extend it from four to eight breaths for even deeper calming effects. This is not a good idea until you know it well, as it might make you slightly light-headed.

Breathe Energy

Throughout history the breath has been associated with energy, force, and power of both a physical and a metaphysical kind. In the Bible, the word translated as "spirit" can also be translated as "air." It is the invisible life force, the energy the Chinese call "chi" and attempt to manipulate in acupuncture treatments. The Sufis refer to it as "baraks." It plays an important role in their techniques of meditation. The yogis call it "prana" and claim it is responsible for the extraordinary control they can exert over their minds and bodies. Prana means breath, respiration, life, vitality, wind, energy, and strength. It is also used to mean soul as distinguished from body. Yogis believe that if we are able to control our breath we can also control pain, emotions, and physical health, as well as supernatural phenomena.

While the act of breathing is supplying your cells with the oxygen they need, it is also removing carbon dioxide and wastes from your system. Carbon dioxide is a by-product of oxidation and energy release. If it were allowed to build up it would poison the cells and eventually kill them. So tiny vessels carry the waste back to the lungs, where it is eliminated when you breathe out and exchanged for new oxygen when you breathe in. At least that is how it should work.

In most people, however, this vital process of taking in necessary oxygen and eliminating poisonous wastes is neither as efficient nor as complete as it should be. This can be due to many things, from tissue anoxia as a result of a diet too high in fats, to insufficient iron, B12, folic acid, or vitamin E, resulting in anemia. But by far the most common cause is simply poor breathing. Most of us use only half our breathing potential and we expel only half the wastes, so in effect we are only getting half the support for health and beauty that we should be getting from oxygen. And because we don't exhale fully, when we take in new air the old air that is still in the lungs is sucked deeper into the alveoli sacs. This means that the oxygen level in the tiny alveoli (which supply the body's bloodstream with oxygen) is far lower than it would be if the air they contained were fresh. Thus the amount of oxygen available to the blood, brain, and nerves, as well as the skin and the rest of the body, is reduced.

On a simpler level, some physicians and therapists such as the late Captain William P. Knowles have had excellent results when treating chronic chest complaints, fatigue, depression, and nervous disorders simply by teaching patients the art of breathing fully. Making changes in the way you breathe or using specific methods of breath control can also help you increase your vitality, calm your emotions when they are disturbed, and clear an overtaxed mind.

The Art of Full Breathing

When you breathe, breathe with your whole chest and abdomen too. Most of us breathe only with the top part of our body, which means we are not fully lowering the diaphragm and expanding the lungs and so are not making use of their full capacity. This kind of restricted breathing stifles emotional expression and is often linked with anxiety, depression, and worry. To check for abdominal breathing, put your hands on your tummy. Does it swell when you breathe in and sink when you breathe out? It should. Lying flat on a firm surface, practice breathing fully and gently until you get the feel of it.

Sensuous Breathing

Lie on the floor on your back and relax as much as you can, letting your arms and legs flop. Close your eyes and feel your body against the floor; do you notice any tension in any part of it? Shoulders? Back? Legs? Now focus inside your body and ask yourself where you feel any movement in your muscles because of your breathing. Anywhere you feel tense, imagine you are breathing into that spot, imagine you can exhale through that part of your body, and as you do, experience the breath relaxing your sore muscles as it filters through them. Then when you are relaxed, experiment with the movements that are part of natural, free breathing. They are beautiful movements.

When you breathe in, feel your pelvis tip back gently so there is a slight arch to your back while your abdomen and chest rise, ribs and back expand, and chin tilts forward just barely. Then, when you exhale, your pelvis moves down again so your spine almost touches the floor, your back contracts, and your chin and head move back again, exposing the front of your neck a bit more. This natural movement is a wavelike motion that flows without hesitation from each in-breath to its following out-breath and so on. Practice it, exaggerating the tiny movements at first until you get the feel of it, and then it will flow naturally.

The Decanter

This exercise stimulates the nervous system and at the same time stills a restless or anxious mind.

Sitting comfortably in a chair with a straight back or cross-legged on the floor, imagine that your body is like a decanter, the bottom of the decanter being your pelvis and hips and the top of it your head. Pretend that you are going to fill it with energy in the form of air. Now, breathing in slowly, imagine it filling up gradually. After you have taken in as much air as you can comfortably hold and are getting to the top, hold your breath as long as necessary to become aware of a feeling of fullness. Then exhale slowly and imagine that the decanter is emptying as you do. Repeat this five to ten times. (If you find yourself becoming light-headed, don't worry. This often happens if the lungs are not used to being fully expanded. But don't ever force your breathing.)

Tension Taker

This exercise is useful to do whenever you find yourself under stress or feel you are getting tense.

Stand comfortably with your arms at your sides and inhale through your nose slowly. Hunch up your shoulders as high as you can, clench your fists, and, standing on tiptoes, tense your body harder and harder, concentrating on your center—the navel area—to help keep your balance. Hold your breath and sink back onto your feet, loosening your shoulders and letting them drop. As you unclench your fists, exhale through your nose very slowly, pushing down through your palms and your shoulders. Do this five or six times.

Prana Power

This is an interesting exercise that uses the breath to do all sorts of surprising things, such as banishing minor aches and pains caused by tension. If practiced regularly it can also help keep the skin of your face looking smooth and wrinkle-free. It is a simple yogic technique for directing prana, or breath energy, to whatever part of your body needs it.

Sitting in a relaxed position with your spine firmly supported, or lying on a firm bed, slowly breathe in deeply, imagining the life force you are taking in as you do. Hold the breath for a few seconds . . . then, as you begin to breathe out, imagine directing the energy to whatever part of your body you want to affect for the better. For instance, see the skin on your face as soft and unlined and direct the energy there, or direct it at your shoulders to make them lose tension, and so forth. Repeat the process for three to five minutes at a time. If you are using it for smoothing away lines on the face, you need to do it twice a day. It is good to do just after a relaxation or meditation exercise if you can.

Guided Imagery: A Vacation Within

We often feel in need of a vacation but commitments may mean we can't take a break. At these times it can be helpful to turn inward and replenish from the resources of the inner world through the imagination. The following guided imagery journey can be recorded on a tape to listen to on a Walkman, perhaps lying in bed.

It is best to do the guided journey lying on your back. If you experience tightness in your lower back with your legs straight, do the exercise with your legs bent, placing your feet near your buttocks, about hip-width apart.

Use the following script to make your own guided imagery tape. Read the text in a slow relaxed way, leaving pauses wherever there are ellipses . . . so that your mind has time to explore each image. You may need a couple of attempts at the recording to get the formula right for you.

Let's begin the journey inward. Make yourself comfortable lying on your back . . . Take a deep breath in and sigh out fully . . . Bring your awareness to the contact between your body and the bed. Allow the bed to support you fully so that your muscles can give up any sense of effort and you can simply enjoy feeling safe, supported, and calm.

Become aware of your breathing. Notice how the air feels as it enters through your nostrils and travels down into your body. Notice the feeling of the air as it leaves your body again. As you inhale imagine that you breathe in peace and relaxation, and as you exhale imagine breathing out any tension or worries . . .

Now imagine that as you inhale the breath travels all the way down to your feet, filling them like balloons. As you exhale the balloons deflate again, leaving your feet completely relaxed and soft. Feel this gentle expansion and deflation in your feet with each breath . . . Now move your awareness to your calves. Again imagine them as balloons. As you breathe in they fill with air and as you breathe out they deflate, becoming loose and limp . . . Enjoy the feeling of calm at the end of an exhalation . . . Now breathe into your knees. Imagine them as small balloons that fill and deflate with the breath . . . Move up to your thighs and allow them to be filled with breath. As you breathe out, let go of any tension so that the thigh muscles become soft and loose . . . Imagine your pelvis as a balloon. As you breathe in feel the balloon expanding all the way around you. As you breathe out, let the balloon collapse. Feel the ease with which the balloon is filled and deflated . . . Now bring your awareness to the balloon of your belly and chest. Feel your ribs expanding as the balloon inflates and as you exhale let the rib cage melt into the bed . . . Now bring your awareness to your hands and let your breath fill them with air. As you exhale feel your hands become soft and loose . . . Let your breath fill the balloons of your lower arms and elbows, leaving your arms limp and heavy on the out-breath . . . Feel the breath in your upper arms and shoulders, loosening any tension as it flows in and leaving your arms and shoulders limp and free as it flows out . . . Now allow your breath to flow gently in and out of your neck and head, bringing a sense of deep relaxation and calm . . . Enjoy the sensation of your breath flowing through your entire body bringing a feeling of peace and contentment to every cell . . .

Now let's begin the journey inward. Become aware of your eyes and imagine them as two pebbles dropping backward toward your inner world. As you follow this movement you find yourself in a tunnel with a point of light ahead of you. You move toward the light and gradually emerge into your inner garden . . .

The landscape is very pleasing to you. It may resemble a place you have already visited or it may be completely new to you. But this garden is part of your own inner world and you feel perfectly at home. Take a moment to admire the surroundings . . .

Winding through the garden is a pathway of soft warm earth. You remove your shoes and begin to walk barefoot along the path, feeling your feet gently massaged beneath you . . . The sun is shining and you feel its warmth on your skin . . . A gentle breeze caresses your face . . . As you walk along the path notice the green of the plants in your garden . . .

You walk through the garden and come to a place that is particularly beautiful. The flowers and trees planted here have been chosen not only for their beauty, but for their fragrances. Notice your favorite flowers . . . Notice which colors are most pleasing . . . Allow the exquisite bouquet of scents to fill your lungs . . .

Soon you hear the sound of running water. As you follow it you come to a small river flowing into a rock pool. It is warm and you decide to bathe in the water. You undress, leaving your clothes on the mossy bank, and step into the pool. The water is invigorating and as it flows over your skin your entire body feels fresh and alive . . .

Flowing into the pool is a stream of pure, clear water that sparkles in the sunlight. You cup your hands under the stream and drink a few sips.

When you are ready, you emerge from the pool onto the bank and notice that some fresh clothes have been laid out ready for you. Notice what color and style they are . . . As you put them on, how does the material feel against your skin? Now look around you for the most comfortable place to sit and relax. Remember this is your garden and you can create anything you like to suit your needs . . . Move to your perfect spot and sit or lie down . . . Allow any thoughts or images to arise spontaneously from this place inside and just enjoy watching them as they do . . .

(Leave a few minutes.)

When you are ready to leave your inner world and come back to the room in which you are lying, simply imagine yourself back in the tunnel of your mind. Let your awareness drift slowly upward toward your eyelids. Take a couple of deep breaths . . . Stretch gently and open your eyes.

CHAPTER 4

Help at Hand

In a world in which the benefits of an invigorating, quick shower are more and more appreci-
ated, it is easy to forget the bliss and the
relaxation of a long lazy bath. Water—especially
when it has been fortified with plant essences—
has the power to soothe, heal, and relax a tense
body, to lift a fatigued spirit, and to put you in
just the right frame of mind for sleep.

Mind–Potions

Allow an hour for the whole process from beginning to end. Make sure you have everything

you need—towel, loofah or hemp glove, and
another towel to use as a headrest. Add essential oils to the water as the bath is filling, using
about ten to fifteen drops total of either a single
essence or a mixture for a large bath. Each
essence has a different effect on the mind
and body. Let them work their wonders while
you carry out a relaxing and waste-eliminating
self-massage. When your bath is finished, lie
down for ten minutes with an eye mask or
a piece of dark fabric across your eyes and
keep warm.

The Massage Message

Water is the perfect medium for self-massage.
The heat (remember not to have your bath too
hot and stimulating) of the water works silent
wonders, and the water supports your body so
that you have easy access to feet, legs, arms,
and torso while still remaining relaxed. When
you get into the bath, gently scrub yourself
all over with a hemp glove or a loofah. Then
just relax and soak for a few minutes, letting
the heat penetrate your muscles. Keep a cool

cloth nearby to smooth over your face when needed.

Now you are ready for massage, which is nothing more than stroking, kneading, pushing, and pressing your skin and muscles. Start with your feet. Grasp one foot between thumb and fingers and press in between the tendons, gently at first, then harder and harder, moving from the toes up toward the ankle. Then, using your fingertips and knuckles, go over the soles of your feet. Wherever you find a sore spot, work harder until you feel the discomfort melt beneath your hand. Now do your heel, grasping it between thumb and fingers and working around the area of the Achilles tendon. This is also a good time to make circles with your foot to loosen the ankle joint. Repeat this with the other foot and then go on to your legs.

Lift each leg in turn and deeply stroke the flesh on the back, from the ankle up to the knee. Then go back to the ankle again and repeat the same motions on the side and front of the calf. Keep working and, as you massage a little deeper with each stroke, you will gradually find that any tautness softens. Now go over your thighs with the same movement and afterward knead and squeeze around the knee

ESSENCE ALCHEMY

As part of the benevolent bath, choose
essential oils not so much for what they can
do for your skin as what they can do to
expand your consciousness and lift your
spirit. Whatever your mental state may be,
it has an enchanting antidote from the
world of flowers:

NEGATIVE STATE	ESSENTIAL OIL REMEDY
anger	ylang-ylang, rose, chamomile
resentment	rose
sadness	hyssop, marjoram, sandalwood
mental fatigue	basil, peppermint, cypress, patchouli
worry	lavender
feeling jaded	neroli, melissa, camphor
feelings of weakness	chamomile, jasmine, melissa
irritability	frankincense, marjoram, lavender, chamomile
physical exhaustion	jasmine, rosemary, juniper, patchouli
anxiety	sage, juniper, basil, jasmine

area wherever there are trouble spots, just as you did on the feet. Now knead each thigh and hip. Then go on to your arms.

Knead and squeeze every spot you can reach on your shoulders and neck, looking for sore spots and focusing on the areas between joints and muscles. Pay particular attention to the tops of the shoulders, where most of us lock away our tension. Grasp this area in your thumb and fingers and insistently ease away any hardness you find there. Finally, go over your ribs, doing each side with its opposite hand.

Hydrotherapy

Water, applied to your body, can "stress" your system in very positive ways—ways that make you stronger and more resistant to illness and that can increase overall vitality. It can improve biological functioning and provide a healthy mental stimulation that takes you away from the habitual ways of thinking that can result in boredom, stress, and sleeplessness.

Sebastian Kneipp, who developed the European system of hydrotherapy, was born in

Bavaria in 1821, the poor son of a humble weaver. His ambition was to become a priest. While studying for the priesthood he contracted tuberculosis. His physicians pronounced him incurable. But Kneipp was unwilling to accept their judgment. He came across an old book written by a German physician on the curative powers of water and began to experiment on himself by applying water in various ways. This, coupled with a growing awareness of the body's own ability to heal itself in accordance with certain laws of nature, brought him back to full health. He went on to develop hydrotherapy into the remarkable therapeutic and preventive system that bears his name.

The following Kneipp techniques are particularly useful for stress or if you find you are unable to get to sleep easily.

Wet Socks

A favorite of Kneipp himself, this is an easy way to apply a foot compress. It is quite extraordinarily relaxing.

Here's how:

Wet a pair of cotton socks in cold water and wring them out so that they are no longer dripping. Put them on and then cover them with a pair of dry wool socks, then pop into bed. Leave the socks on for at least half an hour, although it doesn't matter if they stay on all night should you fall asleep.

Cold Sitz Baths

These last only ten to thirty seconds, according to how quickly and how well you react. They are carried out with the upper part of your body well clothed, always in a warm room. This is also an excellent way of boosting immunity, protecting against minor illnesses (particularly throat and chest conditions), and eliminating flatulence, constipation, and stress.

Here's how:

Fill the bath with enough cold water to reach to your waist. Climb into the bath and stay there for a few seconds, then get out, gently pat the excess water from your skin, and immediately climb into a warm bed.

Herbal Help

Several herbs act as safe and natural tranquilizers that can help relax your mind and body for sleep. One of the most popular is passionflower (*Passiflora*); others include hops, valerian root, and skullcap. You can swallow them in pill or capsule form or make an herbal-tea nightcap. The classic bedtime herbal tea is chamomile, or you could try a tablespoon of orange-flower water stirred into a cup of hot water with a little honey.

• **Valerian:** This is the root of the plant *Valeriana officinalis*, which was the primary herbal sedative used on both sides of the

Atlantic before the advent of barbiturate sleeping pills. It is a safe and well-tested herbal remedy with a smell like dirty old socks (the smell drives some people's cats wild). Don't let that put you off, since valerian is a powerful and useful tool for inducing safe sleep—more potent than most of the other natural tranquilizers such as hops, skullcap, or chamomile.

You can take valerian in a couple of ways but I like the tincture best—ten to twenty drops in a little water before bedtime or in the middle of the night when you awaken. Alternatively you can use a couple of capsules of the dried root. Valerian in lower doses is also useful when your nerves feel "shot" during the day. Very occasionally valerian will be too strong for a particular woman, and she may awaken with a little sense of hangover in the morning. If so you can either cut down on the dose or try another, milder remedy. In any case it can be a good idea to change remedies every so often so your body doesn't become accustomed to one, rendering it ineffectual.

- **Passionflower:** *Passiflora incarnata*, also known as maypops, is a climbing plant that boasts a magnificent white flower with a purple center. It has a wonderful sedative and mildly narcotic effect on the body. Passionflower is most useful for women who wrestle frequently with nervous tension and particularly helpful when nerves seem to be edgy before and around the time of menopause, when hormones can fluctuate wildly. It is also useful for relieving pain thanks to its mild analgesic and antispasmodic qualities—all of which have been well demonstrated in laboratory and clinical tests. Passionflower can also be useful for a woman troubled with premenstrual tension. It is not as strong as valerian in its actions, is more calming than sedating, and as such is a great alternative to tranquilizer drugs. Use ten to twenty drops of the tincture or the same amount of the liquid extract in water. Alternatively take two capsules of the dried extract up to four times a day as needed. (While a woman might take valerian at night just before bed, the best results from passionflower often come from taking it two to four times a day to calm nerves and make everything easier and less stressful.)

- **Chamomile Tea:** One of the nine herbs sacred to the Anglo-Saxon god Wotan, chamomile (*Matricaria camomilla*) was also much loved by the Romans. The Latin name *Matricaria* is derived either from *mater*, meaning mother, or from *matrix*, meaning womb. It has for thousands of years been used as a woman's herb against painful menstruation, to calm anxiety, and to aid sleep—even to help build strong bones, since it contains a form of readily absorbed calcium. Chamomile is also a uterine tonic—something else that has been scientifically evaluated. It boasts many other therapeutic properties as well, such as being antibacterial in its actions and good for skin. The easiest way to take chamomile is in the form of a tisane or tea by infusing five to ten grams of the dried flowers in hot water before bed or whenever you need relaxation. Chamomile works particularly well when taken together with passionflower.

- **Hops:** The flowers from this British herb, *Humulus lupulus*, are often used together with other remedies to treat everything from indigestion to agitated nerves. Like valerian, hops have a pronounced sedative effect, but

are milder. Unlike valerian, hops smell
sweet and can be used without concern
about side effects. You can use hops in the
form of a tincture, but by far the best way for
sleep—particularly good for women who are
awakened in the middle of the night and
have trouble going back to sleep—is to drink
hop tea, which you make before going to bed
by steeping the flowers for ten minutes in
hot water, then straining and allowing to
cool. Put the tea—sweetened with honey if
you like—by the side of your bed so you can
drink it when you awaken in the night. Also
wonderful is a little pillow stuffed with dried
hop blossoms, which you put under your
neck when you go to bed or if you awaken.

- **Oat Straw:** The straw from oats (*Avena
sativa*) has an ability to restore energy when
nerves have been frayed and to counteract
insomnia. It can help ease night sweats,
calm anxiety, and even relieve headache.
Again, stuff a little pillow with oat hulls, or
infuse them in hot water as with hops and
keep a cup beside your bed through the
night in case you need it.

Bedtime Snacks

Although it is best not to go to bed on a full stomach, some people find it helpful to have a little something before retiring. Some foods help promote sleep because they contain high quantities of the amino acid tryptophan—a precursor to the calming brain chemical serotonin—or because they encourage the conversion of tryptophan to serotonin. Others taken at bedtime can disrupt sleep because they stimulate or because they contain high quantities of the chemical tyramine, which increases the release of noradrenaline—a brain chemical that excites the nervous system.

Good sleep foods

Bananas	Tuna
Figs	Whole-grain crackers
Dates	Nut butter
Yogurt	Turkey

Bad sleep foods

Caffeine	Ham
Alcohol	Sausage
Sugar	Eggplant
Cheese	Potatoes
Chocolate	Spinach
Sauerkraut	Tomatoes
Bacon	

Write It Out

You've counted a hundred sheep, told yourself to relax, tried the left side, the right side, the back, the front, turned the light back on, read your book, done the crossword, turned the light off again, and still you're wide awake. Your mind is racing. So why lie there and let it? Rather than try to block all your thoughts out of your head, face them.

Take a pen and some paper and write down all the things that come into your mind. Don't worry if you jump from one thought to another, just keep jotting down thoughts, ideas, and worries. When you run out of things to write you can assure yourself that you can let go of all those concerns for the night because they will be right there on the paper when you wake up.

For several years just before menopause, a good friend of mine awakened each night and would lie silently beside her husband in bed brimming with anger, although she didn't know at what. Finally she decided to get up in the night instead of just lying there. She would go to the kitchen and sit down and write out whatever came to her without even reading what she put down and without trying to make sense of any of it. After several weeks of this she noticed that the anger seemed to become transmuted into new ideas. New plans and solutions to problems would come through her pen. For her, rising from her bed and writing built a bridge between the inner world, which was trying to make itself heard, and the outer, conscious, world in which she lived.

Understanding Sleep

No matter how exhausted you may be at the
end of the day, never be tempted to just flop
into bed. Unless you are relaxed, your sleep
won't be restful and you will have trouble getting out of the right side of bed in the morning.
Sleep is something to be savored and enjoyed,
not something to dash yourself against. Practice relaxation techniques, remember to pam-
per yourself, and take recourse to some of
the helpers, and sleep can be a truly blissful
experience.

Further Reading

If you benefited from this book by health and beauty expert Leslie Kenton, you might like to try the entire series of quick and easy tips for living:

BEAT STRESS (8041-1626-1)
Discover how to identify, then eliminate everyday tension through relaxation, diet, and exercise.

BOOST ENERGY (8041-1625-3)
Increase your stamina and optimize your efficiency by changing your everyday routine.

GET FIT (8041-1628-8)
Develop the best exercise program for your lifestyle, and find out how to stick with it.

LOOK GREAT (8041-1623-7)
Learn the basics for making the most of your appearance by selecting, or creating, effective beauty products.

LOSE FAT (8041-1624-5)
Win the weight war through a simple eating plan that turns food into energy—not fat.

SLEEP DEEP (8041-1627-X)
Get the rest you need with relaxation techniques and healthy, natural sleep potions.

Index